THE NEXUS AMONG TERRORISTS, NARCOTICS TRAFFICKERS, WEAPONS PROLIFERATORS, AND ORGANIZED CRIME NETWORKS IN WESTERN EUROPE

A Study Prepared by the Federal Research Division, Library of Congress under an Interagency Agreement with the United States Government

December 2002

Authors: *Glenn E. Curtis*
Tara Karacan

Project Manager: *Glenn E. Curtis*

Federal Research Division
Library of Congress
Washington, D.C. 20540–4840
Tel: *202–707–3900*
Fax: *202–707–3920*
E-Mail: *frds@loc.gov*
Homepage: *http://www.loc.gov/rr/frd/*

PREFACE

This report describes linkages among narcotics-trafficking, weapons-trafficking, and terrorist activities of groups active in or directly connected with countries in Western Europe. Anecdotal evidence provides examples of transactions among various types of criminal organizations, terrorist organizations, and suppliers of narcotics and arms. Based on that evidence, the report evaluates current trends in such transactions and analyzes the implications and structures of relationships formed by the types of groups under consideration. The report, which covers events and trends of 2000-2002, relies heavily on reports in periodicals. Conclusions have been guided by the work of terrorism and criminology experts such as Tamara Makarenko, Nikos Passas, and Phil Williams.

TABLE OF CONTENTS

KEY JUDGMENTS

- Illegal trafficking in arms and narcotics is increasing in Western Europe, and the patterns of such trafficking are diverse.
- Sources of arms are diverse, but stockpiles in Eastern Europe and the former Soviet Union constitute a major point of origin.
- The majority of illegal weapons proliferation involves individual weapons, but larger weapons also change hands.
- Two major West European terrorist groups, the Basque Fatherland and Liberty organization (ETA) and the Irish Republican Army (IRA) of Northern Ireland have been involved in arms and narcotics trafficking in recent years.
- Both the ETA and the IRA have been linked with narco-terrorist organizations in Latin America, particularly the Revolutionary Armed Forces of Colombia (FARC).
- The Kurdistan Workers' Party (PKK), officially renamed the Freedom and Democracy Congress of Kurdistan, is a Turkey-based terrorist organization with a substantial network that has engaged in terrorist and criminal activity, including narcotics and arms trafficking, in Turkey and Western Europe.
- Arms traffickers and manufacturers in republics of the former Yugoslavia are active suppliers of terrorist groups in Western Europe and elsewhere.
- Belgium and the Netherlands are narcotics trafficking centers where numerous illegal arms dealers have had their headquarters.
- Weapons proliferation tends to be a multi-stage process; once abandoned by a primary user such as the Bosnian Serbs of the mid-1990s, arms return to circulation and "migrate" to new users such as ETA freedom fighters.
- The structure of arms and narcotics transactions is increasingly variable, flexible, and multinational, as are the relations between terrorist and transnational crime groups.

INTRODUCTION

Like many other parts of the world, Western Europe has seen in recent years a notable escalation of illegal trafficking in both narcotics and weapons; the movement of the two types of commodity often is connected or overlapping. The patterns of connection vary greatly, depending on the needs and structures of the criminal groups involved and on the overall national and international context in which they are operating. Flexibility is a key characteristic of most such arrangements. Transnational crime expert Phil Williams points out that arms smuggling often involves institutions and individuals who are not parts of criminal organizations: national defense ministries, national security agencies, banks, legitimate arms dealers, and a wide variety of groups involved in the internal power struggles within nations.[1] Depending on their range of activities and their geopolitical position, groups in the last category may be characterized as "rebel," "guerrilla," or "terrorist."

The same variety of buyers, sellers, and middlemen exists among arms and narcotics smuggling operations. As commercial enterprises, both narcotics and arms sales ultimately are driven by demand. The demand for arms, and the resultant proliferation, has increased with constant expansion of ethnic and regional conflict and of lawless conditions in what Williams calls "states with limited capacities for effective governance."[2] Two major exceptions to that characterization are the Basque region of Spain and France and Northern Ireland, which still host terrorist organizations within nominally well-governed societies. Expansion of narcotics demand has occurred just as rapidly, but most strikingly in the wealthiest nations of the world. Often, symbiotic partners from the narcotics and arms trades straddle the chasm between the two worlds. However, logistical considerations also have brought narcotics and drug trafficking together in the same operations. Says transnational crime expert Michael Chandler,

> The people who are involved in moving drugs are very often the same people who will use the same infrastructure to move human beings as illegal migrants, traffic in weapons, and smuggle any other high-value items. It's like being a good trucker. You don't want to travel the return leg with an empty truck.

---

[1] Phil Williams, "Drugs and Guns," *Bulletin of the Atomic Scientists*, 55, no. 1 (January-February 1999). <http://www.bullatomsci.org>

[2] Williams.

> If you use that sort of analogy, you have drugs coming out one way and that produces money and that buys the weapons and then the weapons go back in.[3]

As it has in the world of legitimate commerce, the globalization of financial, commercial, transportation, and communications networks has enabled buyers and sellers to locate each other, identify points of common interest, and establish terms of cooperation.[4] Western Europe offers a very favorable range of conditions for arms smugglers and narcotics traffickers to accomplish these tasks: a very highly developed and integrated transportation and communications infrastructure and many concentrated urban centers combining large lower-class and immigrant populations with sophisticated commercial operations. Geographically, Western Europe is adjacent to regions such as the Balkans and the former Warsaw Pact states. There, security and police agencies are just beginning to evolve into effective barriers against international trafficking, providing traffickers with smuggling routes still intact from the Soviet period and the lawless 1990s. Globalization also enables criminal groups to take greater advantage of variation among nations in standards and effectiveness of law enforcement.[5]

Western Europe features several varieties of well-established participants in the illicit narcotics and arms trades, including centuries-old Italian crime groups and decades-old national liberation movements such as the Irish Republican Army (IRA) and Basque Fatherland and Liberty (ETA). In recent years, almost all such groups have responded to international police pressure and new opportunities by extending and revising their lines of cooperation. Serving as an example of this adjustment are the Italian criminal groups, who have largely abandoned their previous antipathy toward their Albanian rivals on the eastern shore of the Adriatic Sea in favor of cooperative trafficking ventures that have encompassed most of southern Europe. A generic example of such pragmatism is the increasing tendency for narcotics and arms to be elements of the same transnational trafficking operations. Obviously, criminal and terrorist organizations have recognized the common aspects of their operations: a similarity of underground tactics that can engender short-run trust and understanding, reliance on an increasingly sophisticated range

[3] Robert McMahon, "Afghanistan: UN Official Describes Effort to Track Al-Qaeda," *Radio Free Europe/Radio Liberty*, 28 January 2002. <http://www.rferl.org>

[4] Phil Williams, "Organizing Transnational Crime: Networks, Markets and Hierarchies," in Phil Williams and Dimitri Vlassis, eds., *Combating Transnational Crime: Concepts, Activities and Responses* (London: Frank Cass, 2001), 58.

[5] Williams, "Combating Transnational Crime," 58.

of weaponry and explosives available from transnational dealers, and reliance on international infrastructure systems (financial, commercial, transportation, and communications) offering anonymity and numerous access points. Indicative of this trend is the coining of the term "Euro-crime," which officially includes illegal acts having transnational ramifications in Europe and committed by both terrorist and organized criminal groups.[6] "Marriages of convenience" between the two types of groups expand the possibilities of both, whether driven by profit or by ideology.

One result of these commonalities is a blurring of the distinction between terrorist and criminal groups, most notably in the direction of "fighters turned felons." For example, if narcotics trafficking proves lucrative beyond the immediate goal of paying for arms, the "pure" ideology of a terrorist group such as the ETA may be diluted and some parts of the organization may "wander off" into conventional criminal activity. However, at least two general distinctions remain between the realm of the terrorist and that of the organized criminal. First, for criminal groups profit and risk reduction are the sole motives, while the ideological fire of terrorists may cause them to ignore risk in the short run but to lose focus in the long run. Second, criminal groups rely entirely on defined organization (although contemporary organizational structures show much more variety than "classic" structures), while terrorist acts can be accomplished by individuals or very small groups and terrorist organizations mutate more frequently.[7]

LINKS BETWEEN WEAPONS AND NARCOTICS TRAFFICKING

In the past decade, two major Europe-based terrorist organizations, the IRA and the ETA, have remained at least intermittently active as their political arms sought concessions from the national authorities in their respective homelands. The IRA was founded in 1969 as the armed wing of Sinn Fein, the legal political entity dedicated to removing British forces from Northern Ireland and unifying the country. With periodic cease-fires, the IRA has engaged in assassinations and other forms of attack in Northern Ireland and England since its establishment. In 1994 a small radical splinter group formed, calling itself the Continuity Irish Republican

[6] United Kingdom, Northern Ireland Office, "Crime and Criminal Justice: International Dimensions." <http:www nio.gov.uk/press>
[7] Alison Jamieson, "Transnational Organized Crime: A European Perspective," *Studies in Conflict and Terrorism*, 24, no. 5 (September-October 2001), 394.

Army. Although the main body of the IRA has observed a nominal cease-fire since mid-1997, in the interim a major splinter group calling itself the Real Irish Republican Army (RIRA) has continued to direct assassinations, robberies, and bombings against British military and civilian targets in Northern Island. Authorities believe that the RIRA has had some support from hard-line members of the IRA.[8] In 2002 the Police Service of Northern Ireland estimated the IRA's annual operating budget at US$2.3 million and its fund raising capacity at between US$7.7 million and US$12.3 million.[9]

The ETA was founded in 1959 with the aim of establishing an independent state for the Basque people in northern Spain and southwestern France. Since that time, the ETA has been accused of killing more than 800 people in its terrorist attacks in Spain and France. After having been disrupted substantially in the late 1990s and engaging in a cease-fire in 1999, the ETA reconstituted and streamlined its infrastructure in 2001. By the end of 2001, some 38 more killings were attributed to the group.[10] Like the IRA, the ETA has a substantial political arm that negotiates with state officials and participates in elections. In 1999 the Observatoire Géopolitique des Drogues estimated the ETA's annual budget at between US$15 billion and US$20 billion, much of which was spent to support the organization's legal support structures and exile communities.[11]

Conditions in other areas of the world have promoted arms and narcotics exchanges in Western Europe between criminal groups and terrorist organizations such as the IRA and the ETA. The nearby Balkans have played a central role in the activities of narcotics and arms trafficking groups in Western Europe. In the early 1990s, the fragmentation and breakdown of the central law enforcement system of the former Socialist Federal Republic of Yugoslavia (SFRY) facilitated the activities of criminal trafficking groups. Because law enforcement has remained fragmented and corrupt in most of the region, those patterns of activity continued or accelerated after conventional armed conflict ended in 1995. Criminal groups in all the former

[8] "New Irish Republican Army (NIRA), Real IRA, Óglaigh na hÉireann (Volunteers of Ireland)," FAS Intelligence Resource Program, 2002. <http://www.fas.org/irp/world/para/nira>

[9] Richard Evans, "Organised Crime and Terrorist Financing in Northern Ireland," *Jane's Intelligence Review*, 15 August 2002. <http://www.janes.com>

[10] "Basque Fatherland and Liberty, Euzkadi Ta Askatasuna (ETA)," FAS Intelligence Resource Program, 2002. <http://www.fas.org/irp/world/para/eta>

[11] "World's Drug Traffickers Are Thriving on Globalization, Privatization," Agence France Presse report, 20 April 2000. <http://www.commondreams.org>

republics of the SFRY and in neighboring Albania have participated in various types of trafficking, some of which constitute links between arms and narcotics movements in Western Europe. The dissolution of the Warsaw Pact and the Soviet Union left massive amounts of arms in most of the countries of Eastern Europe and the former Soviet Union. Ineffective inventory monitoring and export controls and official corruption have made such stockpiles available to arms traffickers. Some of those weapons have been exchanged at Western European transit points, particularly in Belgium, and some have remained in the arsenals of West European terrorist groups. Terrorist groups from other parts of the world, especially Asia and Africa, have obtained significant armaments from traffickers based in Western Europe or using Western Europe as part of the delivery route.

IRA Activities

Links between the IRA and the terrorist narcotics group Revolutionary Armed Forces of Colombia (Spanish initialism FARC) have been suspected for some time. However, a major element of that connection was established in August 2001, when Colombian authorities arrested three IRA explosives experts under suspicious circumstances in Bogota. British intelligence reports have estimated that in recent years the FARC has paid IRA operatives about US$2 million for training in arms, explosives, and techniques of urban warfare, using offshore bank accounts; since 1998, between five and fifteen such experts are believed to have moved back and forth between Colombia and Europe. In April 2002, General Fernando Tapas, chief of the Colombian Joint Chiefs of Staff, testified to the House International Relations Committee that in Colombia seven IRA members had trained Colombian, Cuban, Iranian, and perhaps Basque fighters in the use of arms and intelligence for terrorist purposes.[12] The IRA and FARC also may have cooperated in supplying arms to insurgents in Nicaragua in 2000.[13]

Because the IRA strongly discourages individual initiative, all such operatives assumedly have the official approval of the organization. Padraig Wilson, a close associate of Gerry Adams, president of the IRA's political organization, Sinn Fein, is known to have made covert contacts

[12] Andrew Alderson, David Bamber, and Francis Elliott, "IRA's Involvement in International Terrorism," *The Daily Telegraph* [London], 28 April 2002. <http://www nisat.org>
[13] Toby Harndon, "Farc Money Funded Arms Deals," *The Daily Telegraph* [London], 15 May 2002. <http://www.nisat.org>

with FARC in Colombia in the past two years.[14] As of October 2002, the three men who were arrested remained in a Colombian prison with no trial date set.[15]

Such deals offer the IRA two advantages. At a time when the organization is nominally disarming, profits from the Colombian training provide currency with which to tap into the rich assortment of arms available from world traffickers. FARC money may have helped pay for a shipment of 20 highly efficient Russian AN-94 assault rifles that Russian intelligence reported going to the IRA (presumably from corrupt agents in the Russian arms industry or the Russian military) in 2001, at about the same time that the three IRA experts were in Colombia. The IRA also is believed to have purchased arms in Latin America recently.[16] Colombia offers the IRA an inconspicuous area for developing its own weapons and tactics at a time when the IRA nominally is observing a cease-fire in its home territory. On the other side of the deal, the FARC gains training in terrorist and guerrilla techniques from what is widely considered one of the most effective terrorist organizations in the world. The cost is easily affordable, considering that estimates of the FARC's annual narcotics income reach as high as US$1 billion.[17]

Although the links between the IRA and the FARC have not usually constituted direct exchanges of narcotics for weapons, transactions between the two groups have involved both those commodities. The chief income base of the FARC is narcotics sales, and recent IRA payments in narcotics to Croatian arms traffickers (see The Balkan Link) demonstrate that the IRA likely has received narcotics from FARC. The clandestine military training provided to the FARC by the IRA is a form of trafficking that enhances the value of arms acquired elsewhere, and the IRA also may have supplied weapons to the FARC as well: In early 2002, the FARC began using mortars very similar to those designed by weapons expert James Monaghan, one of the three captured IRA agents. According to Colombian authorities, those weapons are a significant upgrade of the FARC's terrorist capability.[18]

---

[14] U.S. Congress, House, International Relations Committee, "Investigative Findings on the Activities of the Irish Republican Army (IRA) in Colombia," 24 April 2002. <http://www neoloiberalismo.com/ira-farc>
[15] Report from Efe News Agency [Spain], 2 October 2002 (FBIS Document EUP20021003000138).
[16] Toby Harnden, "Adams Ally's Trade in Terror," *The Daily Telegraph* [London], 15 May 2002 (FBIS DocumentEUP20020515000149).
[17] Mark Burgess, "Globalizing Terrorism: The FARC-IRA Connection," CDI Terrorism Project report, 5 June 2002. <http://www.cdi.org/terrorism/farc-ira-pr>
[18] Harndon.

Thus the evidence strongly suggests that the IRA is at the center of a complex linkage of narcotics and arms trading that includes criminal groups in Europe and narco-terrorists in Latin America. According to this scenario, the flow of narcotics is mainly from Latin America into Europe, with the IRA using narcotics as currency rather than trafficking actively itself. The more complex flow of arms and arms enhancement services moves from European sources such as Croatian smugglers to the IRA, but it also moves from the IRA to Latin America and vice-versa: the IRA's arms are enhanced by access to FARC testing areas, as the FARC's arms are enhanced by IRA training and arms shipments. The IRA assistance may have been an attempt to upgrade the FARC's capabilities following intensification of United States counter-narcotics assistance that began in 2000.[19]

Other Links in Northern Ireland

Arms trafficking in Northern Ireland is linked to narcotics trafficking in another way as well: of 78 criminal gangs identified by the Police Service of Northern Ireland (RUC) in 2001, some 43 have current or historical links to republican (Catholic) or loyalist (Protestant) paramilitary organizations, including the IRA. Says a 2001 report in *The Guardian*: "Thirty years of terrorism have left a web of networks in which organized crime can thrive and a climate of fear and secrecy that makes fighting such crime very difficult." Such groups take advantage of arms that have been smuggled regularly into Northern Ireland during thirty years of terrorist activity.[20]

According to the RUC, more than two-thirds of gang members are involved in narcotics dealing, 55 percent in forgery and counterfeiting, and 50 percent in money laundering. Groups with loyalist roots tend to be more active in narcotics trafficking than those with republican roots. Loyalist groups normally have granted "franchises" to drug dealers on their territory rather than controlling entire markets themselves. Narcotics trafficking has been especially attractive for newer loyalist groups such as the Loyalist Volunteer Force because narcotics can provide a quick cash return. Interdiction is difficult because police forces have been reduced, are

---

[19] U.S. House of Representatives, Committee on International Relations.

[20] Rosie Cowan, "The 78 Criminal Gangs Waging War on Ulster," *The Guardian* [London], 23 March 2001.

underfunded, and do not enjoy the confidence of the citizenry. In 2001 the police force reported a budget shortfall of 20 million pounds (about US$32 million).[21]

ETA Activities

The ETA has been implicated in narcotics trafficking since at least 1984; ETA groups reportedly have waged wars among themselves to control narcotics markets in Spain.[22] Like the IRA, the separatist ETA is known to use cocaine and heroin to pay for illegal arms shipments in support of terrorist activities. Also like the IRA, the ETA has been linked with arms trafficking operations originating in or transiting through the former Yugoslavia (see The Balkan Link). In 2000 the ETA agreed to supply the Middle Eastern terrorist group Hamas with explosives that the ETA had stolen in Brittany. The deal was an incidental result of a meeting in northern Italy, arranged in the fall of 2000 by a Belgian arms dealer (name unknown) who regularly supplied ETA. Demonstrating the flexibility and complexity of arms trafficking relationships, the ETA attended the meeting not to sell but to purchase arms, having decided to rebuild its supply channels in 1999 after the cease-fire of 1998-99 ended. Several other terrorist groups were present at the meeting, which had the purpose of driving down prices by establishing joint offers to manufacturers.[23] The form of payment for the explosives sold to Hamas is unknown; no narcotics are known to have changed hands.

Italian authorities recently have disclosed information about links between the ETA and the Camorra crime organization based in Naples. By the terms of a 2001 agreement, the Camorra has supplied heavy weapons such as missile launchers and missiles to the ETA in Spain, in return for large amounts of cocaine and hashish. Involved on the Italian side are the Genovese clan, based at Avellino, and several smaller clans in the Torre Annunziata region south of Naples. According to an informant, the initial arrangements of this exchange were made in a face-to-face meeting between a single ETA representative and two representatives of the Italian groups. Subsequently, the Italian groups were represented by Felice Bonneti, a long-time drug

---

[21] Cowan.

[22] Martin Arostegui, "ETA Has Drugs-for-Weapons Deal with Mafia," United Press International report, 3 October 2002. <http://www.washtimes.com>

[23] Carlos Etxeberri, "ETA Sold Part of the Dynamite It Stole During the Cease-Fire to Hamas," *El Mundo* [Madrid], 18 June 2001 (FBIS Document WEU20010618).

trafficker with strong connections in Spain and Italy. Most of the key members of the Italian groups already had "business" connections with the ETA prior to the latest drugs-for-weapons agreement.[24]

The agreement called for heavy arms, explosives, and bombs to be supplied from Pakistan and Uzbekistan via the clans' military contacts in the Czech Republic, 35 to 40 days after delivery of the cocaine. The ETA explicitly refused an offer of Kalashnikov rifles in favor of anti-tank and ground-to-air missiles. Reportedly, the narcotic was delivered weekly to Genoa in special drums attached to the bottom of a ship. Because the investigation of this agreement was announced only in early October 2002, many details are not yet available.[25] Among those details are the original source of the cocaine, actual exchanges that took place before the police learned of the system, and the route (or planned route) followed by any arms and explosives before they reached Spain.

If successful, such an arrangement between the ETA and Italian crime groups would provide the Basque terror organization with arms from the diverse trafficking sources in Eastern Europe and the former Soviet Union, with which the Italian groups seem to be well connected. Although the ETA's drug sources are not directly known, it is likely that the ETA, like the IRA, has an exchange relationship with Latin American narcotics suppliers, by which the ETA moves some of its illegal arms along to narco-terrorist groups in South America in return for narcotics. The arrangement provides the Italian groups another access to Latin American cocaine and hashish, although the Italians complained initially about the quality of the narcotics delivered to them by their ETA partners, according to an informant.[26]

The Balkan Link

Since the Dayton Accords ended fighting between Serbia and Bosnia in 1995, illegal arms trafficking from the Balkans has increased. Arms trafficking routes, already established during the several conflicts that shook the region from 1991 to 1995, expanded as former soldiers

[24] Paolo Chiariello and Gian Antonio Orighi, "ETA and Camorra Crime Syndicate," *Panorama* [Milan], 3 October 2002 (FBIS Document EUP20020927000203); and Martin Arostegui, "ETA Has Drugs-for-Weapons Deal with Mafia," United Press International report, 3 October 2002. <http://www.washtimes.com>
[25] Chiariello and Orighi.
[26] Chiariello and Orighi.

became middlemen, traffickers took possession of stockpiles of arms, and former enemies entered cooperative smuggling ventures.[27] Under these conditions, the former Yugoslav republics of Bosnia-Herzegovina and Croatia have become major sources of illegal arms to both the IRA and the ETA.

The terrorist groups made their connection in Croatia via the Bosnian faction in the Croatian Army, the IM Metal arms and munitions plant in Opal, Croatia, and a group of underworld figures. The latter individuals, who were former members of the French Foreign Legion, were involved in the assassination of Croatian drug trafficking and gambling kingpin Veto Sliško in 2001. According to the report, the IRA and the ETA normally paid for their arms in Colombian cocaine. The Croatian arms dealers, who also trafficked the cocaine they received, were protected by their connections with the Croatian Democratic Union (HDZ), which was the ruling party in the presidency of Franjo Tuđman and continues to be one of Croatia's major political parties. The dealers also had connections with high echelons of Croatia's ministries of defense and internal affairs, customs service, and secret service. Journalist Jasna Babić characterizes this arrangement as "a classic example of a well-organized mafia, composed of classic criminals and portions of the state apparatus."[28] Some Croatian military leaders who emigrated during the war between Croatia and Serbia (1992-93) are known to have participated in IRA operations in the 1990s.[29]

One of the most notorious criminals operating in the northwestern Balkans (Bosnia, Croatia, and Slovenia) is the Tunisian Mohamad bin Saleh bin Hmeidi, known by the sobriquet Carlos. A specialist in narcotics and immigrant trafficking, bin Hmeidi is wanted in several countries for selling weapons to the IRA, the ETA, Islamic organizations, and Italian organized crime groups.[30] No further details of Hmeidi's arms or narcotics transactions are available.

In October 2002, Croatian authorities released four Croatian nationals who had been apprehended in July 2000 with a rocket launcher, antitank weapons, plastic explosives, and

---

[27] Isambard Wilkinson and Julius Strauss, "Karadzić Associates 'Exporting Weapons,'" *The Daily Telegraph* [London], 19 April 2001. <http://www.nisat.org>

[28] Jasna Babić, "MORH [Defense Ministry of Croatia] Protects Arms Dealers Who Smuggle Weapons to ETA and IRA," *Nacional* [Zagreb], 24 July 2001 (FBIS Document EUP20010724000372).

[29] Mario Kavain, "Did Colonel Zulu Arm IRA and ETA Terrorists from the Warehouse at Kaznjenička Battalion? *Jutarnji List* [Zagreb], 18 August 2001 (FBIS Document EUP20010820000136).

[30] Hassan Haidar Diab, "Panic in Slovenia Due to Possible Release of Josip Lončarić," *Večernji List* [Zagreb], 21 November 2001 (FBIS Document EUP20020502000202).

ammunition allegedly destined for the Real IRA, a splinter group of the IRA. Although at the time of the arrest authorities claimed to have broken a major arms smuggling ring whose existence was known as early as 1997, the suspects finally were released for lack of evidence.[31] A shipment of Wasp rockets, known to be a favorite weapon of the Real IRA, was confiscated in Slovenia at the same time as the Croatian discovery was made. Although authorities believe that the shipments in Croatia and Slovenia were part of a larger chain, they never were able to confirm the connection. Arms orders allegedly passed to Croatia from the ETA and the IRA through a criminal group in France.[32] In 2000 European authorities discovered an attempt by the ETA to buy Croatian arms from the IRA.[33]

In 2001 a Spanish documentary asserted that the IRA and other terrorist groups in Europe were buying a wide variety of weapons and munitions from an arms trafficking gang based in the Serbian Republic of Bosnia and Herzegovina. The arms come from Yugoslav and Bosnian military and police units and are sold by a relative of Radian Koradji, a former Bosnian Serb leader who is wanted for war crimes in Bosnia by the Hague Tribunal. The journalists, posing as agents of Colombian narcotics dealers, located a stockpile of former Bosnian Serb army weapons in Sokolac, Bosnia, by contacting first a Croatian gangster in Spain, then a series of organized crime contacts in the Balkans. Included in the arsenal were hollow-tipped bullets and bullets carrying chemicals, both of which are banned by international law. The dealers requested payment half in cash and half in cocaine for a large shipment of rifles, machine guns, pistols, explosives, ammunition, and grenades.[34]

French and Spanish authorities have established a positive linkage of Croatian arms and explosives with the ETA. Beginning in 1998, French authorities have captured shipments of explosives, anti-personnel mines, handguns, and grenades originating in Croatia and bound for Basque territory. The military pistol that Basque terrorists used to kill Aragon Popular Party president Manuel Gimenez Abad in Spain was manufactured by the Ožalj plant south of Zagreb. The barrel of that gun model originates in Germany and its ammunition in the Czech Republic.

---

[31] Ivo Scepanovic, "Arms Smuggling: Four Suspects Released," reported in *The Irish News* [Belfast], 17 October 2002 (FBIS Document EUP20021017000122).
[32] Kavain.
[33] Arostegui.
[34] Giles Tremlett, "Northern Ireland Special Report: War Crimes in the Former Yugoslavia," *The Guardian* [Manchester], 5 April 2001, reported by Norwegian Initiative on Small Arms Transfers. <http://www.nisat>

Large, undeclared shipments of those barrels also have been intercepted on Croatia's borders in recent years, and the distinctive military pistol has been found on black markets in Austria, Slovenia, and Spain. This evidence indicates that Ožalj likely is a major source of small arms to criminal groups in Europe and, possibly, elsewhere. Despite substantial evidence linking Ožalj with the ETA, Croatian authorities charged the plant only with customs violations—selling arms on the European black market—rather than with smuggling arms to a terrorist organization. ETA was not mentioned in the final charges brought in 2001.[35]

The ETA also is known to have sold explosives and money laundering expertise to the FARC and the IRA in the late 1990s, although the individuals who delivered these services technically had left the organization. Using connections with domestic and regional organized crime, the ETA also has sold money-laundering techniques to drug traffickers in Spain and used traditional smuggling networks to sell narcotics and deliver money to laundering institutions in Switzerland and elsewhere.[36]

Other European Links

In late 2001, European intelligence sources reported significant activity by Italian and other European crime organizations in smuggling arms to Palestinian groups in the Middle East. This is a continuation of a linkage that has existed for at least a decade; in 1992, Italian authorities reported connections between Italian crime groups and the government of Syria. In that relationship, the Italians sold narcotics to purchase weapons that were sold to various Arab clients through the Syrian government.[37] Through Arab intermediaries in several countries, Italian groups have offered to sell a wide variety of heavy weapons and ensure their delivery at a price below standard international rates. The two routes for such negotiations have been Brussels-to-Beirut and Milan-to-Beirut. Among the weapons for sale are the French-made Milan guided missile and smaller weapons made in Belgium. European mafia organizations also

[35] Babić.
[36] Observatoire Géopolitique des Drogues, *The World Geopolitics of Drugs 1998-1999: Annual Report.* (Dordrecht: Kluwer, 2001), 127.
[37] Williams, "Drugs and Guns."

reportedly have been in contact with the Free Lebanese Resistance, a group dedicated to freeing Lebanon from Syrian control.[38]

According to recent reports, Greece is an important transit point for the international arms trafficking industry. Albanian, Italian, and Russian organized crime groups and guerrilla organizations in Kosovo are moving arms through various parts of Greece to points elsewhere in Europe.[39] Greek security authorities estimate that 50,000 illegal guns per year enter Greece.[40] In August 2001, a Greek newspaper report stated, "guns and narcotics are shipped to Greece from nations of the former USSR and are then shipped to European nations through Italy. The immense profits of this trade are laundered in Greece and Cyprus, where the Russian mafia has a strong support base. The Russian mafia is also involved in narcotics and prostitution." Interdiction has been difficult because Russian groups have established links with "influential officials" in Greece.[41] Another important source of illegal arms trade in Greece is the large number of weapons (estimated at 550,000) stolen from military stockpiles in Albania during that country's 1997 uprising.[42]

In Greece the illegally traded weapons are primarily light guns, including the Russian Kalashnikov and the Israeli Uzi, although items such as rocket launchers also appear on the black market. Sicilian mafia groups have been trafficking in cigarettes, arms, and narcotics in western Greece since at least 1999. This trade often is done in cooperation with Albanian groups, which by the 1990s already had begun exploiting Greece's northwestern coastline with high-speed boats.[43] Romanian groups also have a share of the market in Athens.[44]

Crete is the largest center of the arms trade, but Albanian traffickers have established significant markets in the Evros River delta and in the city of Ioannina, in northeastern and northwestern Greece respectively. Kalashnikovs and grenades from Albania often remain in the

---

[38] Murray Kahl and Naji N. Najjar, "The Syrian Mafia Connection," Lebanese Foundation for Peace report, 7 November 2001. <http://www free-lebanon.com>

[39] V. Nikolakopoulos, "The Arms Trade in Greece," *Vima tis Kiriakis* [Athens], 5 August 2001, cited in International Action Network on Small Arms. <http://www.iansa.org>

[40] Yeoryios Sombolos, "2.5 Billion Drachmas Annual Turnover from Arms Trafficking," *Imerisia* [Athens], 22 December 2001. <http://www nisat.org>

[41] Nikolakopoulos.

[42] Sombolos.

[43] Kostas Khatzidis, "The Italian Mafia Has Spread Its Tentacles into Greece," *Ta Nea* [Athens], 20 July 2000. <http://www.nisat.org>

[44] "Romanian Arms Traffickers Take Over Athens Market," *VIMAgazino* [Athens], cited in *Ziua* [Bucharest], 10 August 2001. <http://www nisat.org>

hands of crime organizations in Greece. Smuggled weapons also enjoy a substantial market among ordinary Greeks because of Greece's onerous gun ownership requirements.[45]

Belgium, which until 2000 was the primary weapons source for the ETA,[46] also has significant trafficking activity. It has been linked with the names of several individuals known to smuggle large amounts of illegal arms to areas outside Europe, especially Africa. United Nations arms specialist Johan Peleman reports that a large arms-trafficking infrastructure appeared in Belgium because of the international diamond-trading center in Antwerp (also a major narcotics transit port)[47] and the post-colonial ties that Belgium retained with Africa. When the Cold War ended, arms trafficking networks changed hands among private entrepreneurs rather than being disbanded; Peleman estimated that in the mid-1990s as many as ten such networks were operating in the port city of Ostend alone.[48]

Peleman has theorized that Belgium is not the only West European former African colonial power so deeply involved in arms trafficking. He notes that "if Portugal were to undertake an analysis, that country would also realize that all those old networks which attempted to put a brake on decolonialization, which built up groups of mercenaries and traffickers—in Angola, Mozambique, etc.—are still in existence. And it is the same people who are involved in the trafficking of arms and of diamonds."[49] Diamonds also have been instrumental in arms trafficking to other parts of the world; in 2000, Belgian authorities identified diamonds as the exchange currency in shipments to the Middle Eastern terrorist organization Hezbollah.[50] Although not specifically linked to the narcotics trade, such trafficking operations, which have stood the test of time and political change, also have the potential to diversify their clientele and the currency that they accept in payment. Several individuals have based especially lucrative arms smuggling operations in Belgium.

The Tajikistan-born Victor Bout (Viktor Butt) has been accused of supplying arms originating in Russia and Eastern Europe to rebel forces in several African countries and to

---

[45] Sombolos.
[46] Report in *El Mundo* [Madrid], 20 March 2001 (FBIS Document WEU-20010320). <http://www nisat.org>
[47] "Belgian Police Seize Three Tons of Cocaine," VRT radio broadcast, Brussels, 1 July 2002 (FBIS Document EUP20020701000365).
[48] Interview with Johan Peleman in *Le Soir* [Brussels], 7 March 2002.
[49] Interview with Johan Peleman.
[50] "UN Investigates Links of Belgian Diamond Dealers with Afghan Terrorism," *Le Soir* [Brussels], 14 March 2002, reported by Norwegian Initiative on Small Arms Trafficking. <http://www nisat.org>

terrorist groups including al-Qaeda. Until he moved to the United Arab Emirates in 1997, Bout's base of operations was Ostend, Belgium. Bout now has branch "offices" in several other countries, including Kazakhstan, Dubai, Gibraltar, and Zimbabwe, as well as a large fleet of transport aircraft. His Air Cess air transport company and Transaviation Network Group retain their headquarters in Ostend. A typical delivery mission to Africa picked up arms in Burgas, Bulgaria, stopped in Togo to establish the official destination of the shipment, and unloaded in Liberia. The arms then went overland to rebels in Sierra Leone.[51] In February 2002, Belgium issued an international warrant for Bout's arrest. Bout has no known involvement with narcotics; his African transactions have been financed by diamonds and minerals from the African countries of destination. In February 2002, authorities arrested four Bulgarian residents of Belgium, allegedly working for Bout. The charge was arms trafficking in Angola and laundering US$50 million in profits from that trade. Evidence also indicated a possible link with the Taliban.[52]

Bout's Air Cess company also used his base at Sharjah in the United Arab Emirates (UAE) to cooperate with the Taliban-controlled Ariana Airlines and the locally owned Flying Dolphin Airlines to move arms to the Taliban and thus to al-Qaeda. Bout's base in Sharjah took advantage of the UAE's lax banking transparency and import-export laws. Although Bout's link with al-Qaeda nominally has been cut by the UAE's enforcement of the international ban on arms to Afghanistan since 2001, Bout's activities and whereabouts still were not clear as of late 2002.[53]

Until his arrest in Italy in mid-2001, Ukrainian-born Leonid Minin was another major link between corrupt arms sources in Eastern Europe and the former Soviet Union and rebel armies and corrupt leaders in sub-Saharan Africa. Based in northern Italy and receiving documentation in Belgium, Minin specialized in delivery of Kalashnikov rifles, rocket-propelled grenades and launchers, ammunition, and specialized combat equipment in return for precious gems. A typical delivery took 68 tons of small arms and ammunition via Antonov-124 military transport from Ukraine to the shipment's official destination, Burkina Faso. The shipment then

---

[51] Report in *Le Vif/L'Express* [Brussels], 2 March 2002.
[52] "Ring, Possible Links with Taliban," *Le Soir* [Brussels], 9 February 2002. <http://www nisat.org>
[53] Judy Pasternak and Stephen Braun, "Following the Trail of Arms to Al-Qaida," *Los Angeles Times*, 21 January 2002. <http://www.nisat.org>

was transported on Minin's private jet to Liberia, for subsequent delivery to rebel forces in Sierra Leone. End user certificates specifying the Burkina Faso military as recipient provided cover for the Ukrainian government officials who licensed the shipment. Reportedly, Russia, Belarus, and Bulgaria are equally important points of origin for such shipments,[54] and Minin has used connections with former KGB officials to gain access to Russian stockpiles.[55] Like Bout, Minin apparently received payment for his arms mainly in precious gems; no link has been established between Minin's arms trafficking and narcotics traffickers, although Minin is known to be a heavy user of cocaine.

The Belgian Jacques Monsieur also based an active arms smuggling enterprise in Belgium in the 1990s. Monsieur moved arms from Russia, the Czech Republic, Poland, and Bulgaria to Angola and various other African states, allegedly with support from the French oil giant Elf Aquitaine. In October 2002, Monsieur returned to Belgium to stand trial for arms smuggling; he also is wanted in France.[56] Authorities also linked Monsieur with the sale of French missiles and artillery shells to a Croatian trafficking group for use in Balkan conflicts between 1991 and 1993.[57] Like Bout and Minin, he has no known connection with narcotics trafficking.

The Netherlands also offers conditions favorable to illegal trafficking: a highly developed communications system and two major seaports, Amsterdam and Rotterdam, where a high volume of cargo containers is handled quickly and with relatively lax import-export controls.[58] Amsterdam's Schiphol Airport also is a European center of narcotics and human trafficking, allegedly because of lax security controls.[59] These conditions, which have made the Netherlands one of the most active narcotics transfer countries in the world, also are favorable to arms trafficking.

---

[54] Ian Traynor, "The Gunrunner," *The Guardian* [Manchester], 9 July 2001.
[55] Report of Radio France Internationale, 19 June 2002 (FBIS Document AFP20020619000123).
[56] Marc Metdepenningen, "Jacques Monsieur Hopes for Release," *Le Soir* [Brussels], 12 October 2002 (FBIS Document EUP20021013000011); and Alaian Lallemand, "A Belgian Angolagate?" *Le Soir* [Brussels], 16 June 2001 (FBIS Document EUP20010617000081).
[57] Patrick Bishop, "French Spy Service 'Broke UN Embargo,'" Norwegian Initiative on Small Arms Transfers, 12 June 2001. <http://www.nisat.org>
[58] Stephane Alonso, "Fight Against Narcotics is Symbolic," *NRC Handelsblad* [Rotterdam], 31 August 2002 (FBIS Document EUP20020902000252).
[59] Steven Derix and Jos Verlaan, "Investigative Services Want More Operational Powers at Schiphol," *NRC Handelsblad* [Rotterdam], 29 July 2002 (FBIS Document EUP20020730000226).

In recent years, authorities in Amsterdam have reported significantly increased activity by crime groups from the Balkans and Turkey. These groups specialize in smuggling immigrants, narcotics, and arms. Showing some specialization (Turkish groups have focused on narcotics, Slavic groups on arms), the groups have fought over markets and territories in the city. Police raids have found grenade launchers, explosives, and "heavy weapons suitable for warfare," believed to be in transit from origins in Eastern Europe to terrorist groups. No specific group was named as a likely recipient of these arms. Dutch authorities have found heroin, counterfeit money, and jewels together with the arms.[60]

Military stockpiles and legal arms manufacturers in Croatia and Slovenia are important sources of smaller arms to the active Amsterdam illegal arms market. Small machine guns are a specialty of Croatian manufacturers. Prior to the NATO bombardment of Serbia's arms plants in 1999, that country also was a significant provider to this market. Dutch authorities have identified some arms traffickers from the republics of the former Yugoslavia as narcotics traffickers as well, at least on a limited scale.[61]

The PKK/KADEK

The Turkey-based Kurdistan Workers' Party (Partiya Karkaren Kurdistan, PKK—renamed in 2001 the Freedom and Democracy Congress of Kurdistan, KADEK) is a terrorist organization with various illegal trafficking and money-laundering activities that depend heavily on links in Western Europe. Because it is known to have dealt extensively with criminal organizations in trafficking both arms and narcotics, the PKK has been an important nexus of criminal activities with terrorism.[62] The group's scope of terrorist operations has been significantly reduced since the arrest of its leader, Abdullah Öcalan, in 1999.

The PKK was founded in 1974 as a Marxist-Leninist insurgent group consisting mainly of Kurds living in Turkey. The organization's original goal was to establish a Kurdish state in southeastern Turkey, where about half of the world's 30 million Kurds live with arguably

---

[60] Marlise Simons, "Balkan Gangs Stepping Up Violence, Dutch Say," *New York Times*, 30 November 2000. <http://www.nisat.org>

[61] Jos Verlaan, "Yugos Dominate Netherlands Arms Market," *NRC Handelsblad* [Rotterdam], 5 July 2002 (FBIS Document EUP20020708000079).

[62] T. Roule, "The Terrorist Financial Network of the PKK," *Jane's Terrorism and Security Monitor*, 17 June 2002.

insufficient recognition of their status. In recent years, that goal has changed from independence to autonomy for Kurds within the Turkish state. The reaction of the government of Turkey has been severe repression, based on the assertion that Kurdish autonomy is a threat to the indivisibility of the state. From 1988 to 1998, the PKK confronted Turkey with what some experts rated the most serious terrorist threat in the world, graduating in the early 1990s from rural insurgency to highly effective urban terrorism that included suicide bombings. Attacks have targeted both Turkish security forces and civilians (often, Kurds accused of cooperating with the Turkish state). The group also has attacked Turkish targets in Western Europe.[63] The government of Turkey claims that between 1988 and 1998 the PKK killed more than 25,000 Turks, mostly in attacks launched within Turkey. At the same time, the PKK was engaging in narcotics trafficking, arson, blackmail, and extortion in many West European countries.

Although PKK leader Abdullah Öcalan declared a "peace initiative" after his capture in 1999 and the organization has claimed recently to be transforming itself from a militant group into a political movement, the organization has remained active enough for Turkish security forces to conduct major cross-border operations against it in northern Iraq, where the majority of PKK members have taken refuge, in late 2001.[64] In November 2002, eleven Turkish soldiers died in another military operation in Iraqi Kurdistan. However the same month the Turkish government ended the 15-year state of emergency that had been established in southeastern Turkey in response to the PKK's activities. Although in 2002 no terrorist incidents were attributed to the PKK, experts believe that the supportive structure of its criminal activities remains in place. According to a recent report, "an analysis of PKK funding indicates the PKK is adopting patterns of behavior similar to the Philippine-based Abu Sayyaf group, which eschews civic and cultural duties and concentrates attention on criminal activities to sustain a small, but threatening, military presence.[65]

The PKK has funded its terrorist activities from a number of illegal enterprises, including the trafficking of narcotics and people, combined with voluntary and forced contributions from the Kurdish diaspora. In Europe, regional criminal organizations parallel terrorist and political

---

[63] Federation of American Scientists, Intelligence Resource Program, "Kurdistan Workers' Party (PKK)." <http://www.fas.org/irp/world/para/pkk>
[64] Federation of American Scientists, Intelligence Resource Program.
[65] Roule.

cells and have common membership.[66] Some of the group's illicit profits come from a sophisticated people-smuggling network that transports refugees from northern Iraq to Italy. The three most frequently used routes for this movement are Istanbul-Milan, Istanbul-Bosnia-Milan, and Turkey-Tunisia-Malta-Italy. In the 1990s, the PKK also was identified with significant amounts of international arms smuggling. According to anecdotal evidence, the PKK supplied arms to other Kurdish terrorist groups and to the Tamil Tigers of Sri Lanka.[67] Banks in Belgium, Cyprus, Jersey, and Switzerland provide privacy for PKK funds; monetary transactions are done through the *hawala* system or by cash couriers.[68]

The most profitable illegal activity, however, has been narcotics trafficking. Germany's chief prosecutor asserted that 80 percent of narcotics seized in Europe have been linked to the PKK or "other Turkish groups," which then have used the profits from illegal narcotics to purchase arms.[69] Apparently this statistic combines the PKK with other Kurdish and ethnic Turkish criminal groups, which also are very active in sending narcotics into Western Europe. For this reason, the PKK's true share of the narcotics market in Western Europe cannot be ascertained precisely. Experts agree, however, that the PKK has benefited handsomely from the location of Kurdistan in the far southeastern corner of Turkey, closest to the major narcotics sources of South Asia and Central Asia. This location has allowed it to play a major role in moving drugs westward. The organization's narcotics activities connect it with major criminal groups in Istanbul and with high officials in the Turkish government.[70]

A variety of agencies, including the U.S. Department of State, the U.S. Drug Enforcement Administration, the United Nations International Drug Control Programme, and the Observatoire Géopolitique des Drogues, have documented the PKK's high level of narcotics trafficking throughout the 1990s.[71] During that decade, the International Police Organisation

---

[66] See, for example, the description of the relationship of the two activities in Germany in "Indictment of Two Alleged PKK Functionaries," announcement of federal prosecutor's office, Karlsruhe, Germany, 29 October 2002 (FBIS Document EUP20021029000049).
[67] Turkey, Ministry of Foreign Affairs, "Greece and the PKK Terrorism." <http://www mfa.gov.tr>
[68] Roule.
[69] Radu Tudor, "The Drugs Mafia Finances the Terrorist Organization in Romania," *Ziua* [Bucharest], 11 February 2002 (FBIS Document EUP20020211000247).
[70] Roule.
[71] "PKK's Involvement in Drug Trafficking." <http://www kbl.tr>

(Interpol) followed the narcotics smuggling activities of several Kurdish clans based in Germany, Italy, the Netherlands, and Spain and thought to have ties with the PKK.[72]

According to Turkish security expert Ali Koknar, PKK cooperation with Kurdish criminal clans has been similar to the cooperation among Sicilian mafia families. The PKK is a multilevel business organization that is involved in all phases of the narcotics trade, from production to retail distribution. The first phase is laboratory production from a morphine base, usually obtained from Pakistan; the final phase is sale on the street in Europe through pushers employed by the organization. The PKK is known to operate laboratories in Turkey and northern Iraq. Distribution networks also are used to sell ready-made heroin, morphine base, cannabis, and anhydride acid, a raw material imported into Turkey from Germany for heroin production.[73] Besides trafficking done by individual cells to support their operations, the PKK also "taxes" ethnic Kurdish drug traffickers in Western Europe.[74]

CONCLUSION: STRUCTURES AND IMPACT OF ARMS AND NARCOTICS INTERACTION

Structures

Although illegal trafficking in arms frequently coexists with illegal trafficking in narcotics, the two activities do not necessarily have a symbiotic relationship; rather, conditions that promote one type of trafficking very often promote the other. Thus organized crime groups in Italy, Albania, and the former Yugoslavia trade in both types of commodity, taking advantage of available resources as well as favorable conditions. Often, narcotics and arms are items of exchange in a complex deal that involves third and fourth parties. More rarely, arms and narcotics are the two components of a simple, direct exchange between a criminal and a terrorist group, as in the case of the Italian crime group's recent exchange with the ETA of arms for narcotics.

[72] "PKK's Drug Trafficking Is Organised by Kurdish Tribes Having Organic Ties with PKK," report of International Affairs News Agency [Ankara], February 1997. <http://www.inaf.gen.tr>

[73] Gunduz S. Aktan and Ali M. Koknar, "Turkey," in Yonah Alexander, ed., *Combating Terrorism: Strategies of Ten Countries* (Ann Arbor: University of Michigan Press, 2002), 291.

[74] Randy Beers and Francis X. Taylor, "Narco-Terror: The Worldwide Connection Between Drugs and Terror," testimony before Senate Committee on the Judiciary, Subcommittee on Technology, Terrorism, and Government Information, 13 March 2002.

Almost always, however, such exchanges are made at one stage of an extended route followed by the respective commodities. For example, one of the direct IRA narcotics-for-arms exchanges with Croatian arms dealers began on one side with acquisition of narcotics by the FARC from a drug cartel in Colombia and on the other side with acquisition of arms by mafia middlemen from a source in Eastern Europe or the former Soviet Union. The IRA may be the final user of the arms, or it may trade some of them to the FARC for additional narcotics. On the other side, the Croatians likely will sell the narcotics on the domestic or foreign market. Such complexity is especially characteristic of transactions based in Western Europe, which offers multiple opportunities and multiple commodities to criminal entrepreneurs.

Because both criminal and terrorist activity thrive in unstable political conditions, associations between the two have appeared most often in the "developing world" rather than in Western Europe or North America.[75] However, the latter regions have major narcotics markets, optimal infrastructure, and "wide-open" commercial nodes that increasingly serve the transnational trafficking needs of both criminal and terrorist groups. Those factors, combined with the continued existence of major terrorist organizations in the United Kingdom, France, and Spain, and available stockpiles of military supplies in Eastern Europe, have made Western Europe a key junction point.

The overlapping and cooperation of the activities of organized crime groups and terrorist groups has increased in recent years. This change is partly because formal state sponsorship of terrorism began to decrease when the Cold War ended, forcing terrorist groups to find alternative sources of financial support. Association of the two types of groups has occurred in three broad patterns. The first pattern is alliances for mutual benefit, in which terrorists enter agreements with transnational criminals solely to gain funding, without engaging directly in commercial activities or compromising their ideologically based mission. This arrangement normally has been the first form of contact between the two types of group. The second pattern is direct involvement of terror groups in organized crime, removing the "middleman" but maintaining the ideological premise of their strategy. The third pattern is the replacement of ideology by profit as the main motive for operations. The line between the second and third patterns is difficult to

[75] Makarenko, "Systematic Transnational Crime."

distinguish because self-styled insurgents/terrorists fear that if they are perceived to have rejected their ideology, they will lose popular support.[76]

Most of the terrorist groups described in this report follow most closely the second pattern. They have been willing to engage directly in the sale of various commodities, including arms, narcotics, and people, as well as the laundering of their profits, to support ideological goals. Few major groups have been content to rely exclusively on the entrepreneurial activities of organized criminal partners, remaining above direct participation in the global market for illicit commodities. A natural progression seems to occur from the first category toward the third. The main reason for movement away from the first category is the sheer complexity of most lines of transnational exchange of illegal commodities. This complexity means that few partners can expect to be the end recipients of precisely what they were seeking from the market, with no collateral transactions. If the availability of Kalashnikovs to the ETA depends on the status of another transaction between Bulgarian arms sellers and international arms merchant Victor Bout, the ETA customer must be aware of possible outcomes. Contact with such an atmosphere causes ideological terrorists to think as "businessmen" at least within the context of a particular deal. Contemporaneous transnational criminal organizations have proven the value of flexibility, mobility, and pragmatism.[77] In such an atmosphere, even terrorists with strong ideologies are tempted to "diversify," especially if diversification eases the way for a new shipment of Kalashnikovs or explosives. Association with successful transnational criminal operations also may convey to terrorists the idea that handsome profits are available to those who are pragmatic rather than doctrinaire.

The same forces have pushed at least parts of some terrorist organizations fully into the third category, that of fighters-turned-felons. Such a change is especially likely if the original internal disciplinary structure of the group has begun to erode through practices such as the skimming of profits from criminal activities.[78] Such a change is less likely in organizations with the following conditions: an active, charismatic leader such as Osama bin Laden; an large, multinational following; and minimal compromising of the cause by cease-fires and political

[76] Makarenko, "Systematic Transnational Crime."
[77] See especially the discussion of this subject in Phil Williams, "Organizing Transnational Crime: Networks, Markets and Hierarchies."
[78] Evans.

negotiations such as those undertaken by the ETA and the IRA. Organizations (or, more commonly, factions of organizations) that enter the third category are able to apply lessons learned and networks developed in a previous incarnation in category one or category two. Tamara Makarenko points out that, once a group enters category three, "instability is sustained for the sole purpose of profit-seeking." As an example, Makarenko suggests that the splinter RIRA's ongoing terrorist activities, done in the name of continuing the cause deserted by the parent organization's peace efforts, actually aim to preserve the environment of instability that protects the group's criminal activities. In other parts of the world, groups following the same pattern in recent years have been the FARC, the Kosovo Liberation Army (KLA), and the Islamic Movement of Uzbekistan (IMU).[79]

Impacts

Police reports and other anecdotal evidence indicate that the rate of arms trafficking across Western Europe has increased in the last three years (2000-02), despite a series of cease-fires involving key regional terrorist groups. In that period, the ETA and the IRA have taken advantage of ready supplies of illegal weapons to enhance their stockpiles. In many cases, such purchases have been linked with organized crime groups acting as middle-men. Western Europe also functions as a transit area for arms moving from the former Soviet Union and Eastern Europe to conflict points in Africa and Asia.

Experts agree that recent events in the linkage between the Real IRA and the Colombian FARC guerrilla group can significantly upgrade the capabilities of the FARC, which in 2001 already was the most powerful terrorist group in Colombia and controlled an estimated 40 percent of the country. Of particular potential value was training in the design of explosive devices and the use of mortars and rockets—subjects in which the "Bogota Three," who were arrested in 2001, were expert.[80] Thus the Irish connection enhanced FARC's existing armaments by improving their application. In turn, the increased effectiveness of the FARC as a paramilitary organization protects it from domestic interdiction, enhancing the group's dissemination of narcotics in international markets.

---

[79] Makarenko, "Systematic Transnational Crime."

[80] Jeremy McDermott and Toby Harnden, "The IRA and the Colombian Connection," *Daily Telegraph* [London], 15 August 2001, reported by Norwegian Initiative on Small Arms Transfers. <http://www.nisat.org>

In Northern Ireland, illegal arms imports, often financed directly or indirectly by narcotics, have had a domestic impact beyond the immediate confrontation between terrorists and authorities. First, the long-term presence of terrorist groups has spawned a large number of criminal groups. In turn, the activity level and social threat of those groups has increased because their links to terrorist groups give them access to more sophisticated arms than they would have otherwise. Coupled with an ineffective police force, this situation "threatens the development of normal civilised society" in Northern Ireland.[81]

The heavy weapons confiscated in Croatia and Slovenia in mid-2000 indicate that the RIRA was contemplating escalation of its attacks in Northern Ireland after a lull in 1998-99. The availability of a great variety of arms through international trafficking and the narcotics connections that ease payment provide terrorist groups the option of making such tactical changes when they consider them necessary. Often, the addition of larger weapons such as anti-tank guns has signaled a terrorist group's change of emphasis to attacking hard military installations rather than civilian targets, which can be reached with less sophisticated explosive devices. However, an escalation to surface-to-air missiles (such as one that the ETA was suspected of buying in 2001)[82] may indicate that civilian aircraft have become a target.

The demand for illegal weapons in Western Europe has supplemented the demand in Africa and Asia that has supported trafficking networks that base their operations on stockpiles in the former Warsaw Pact nations, the former Yugoslavia, and the nations of the former Soviet Union. This demand, which is based both in terrorist groups and in organized crime networks, ultimately benefits both corrupt military and civilian operators in source countries such as Bulgaria, Ukraine, Russia, and Romania, and intermediary agents such as Albanian, Croatian, Romanian, and Serbian criminal groups. The ongoing world demand for military-type weapons has slowed efforts by struggling countries such as Bulgaria and Romania to dispose of their military surpluses in less lucrative but more socially beneficial ways.

[81] Rowan.
[82] Report in *El Mundo* [Madrid], 20 March 2001 (FBIS Document 20010320000374).

BIBLIOGRAPHY

Aktan, Gunduz S., and Ali M. Koknar. "Turkey." Pages 260-298 in Yonas Alexander, ed., *Combating Terrorism: Strategies of Ten Countries.* Ann Arbor: University of Michigan Press, 2002.

Alderson, Andrew, David Bamber, and Francis Elliott. "IRA's Involvement in International Terrorism," *The Daily Telegraph* [London], 28 April 2002. <http://www.nitas.org>

Alexander, Yonah, ed. *Combating Terrorism: Strategies of Ten Countries.* Ann Arbor: University of Michigan Press, 2002.

Alonso, Stephane. "Fight Against Narcotics Is Symbolic," *NRC Handelsblad* [Rotterdam], 31 August 2002 (FBIS Document EUP20020902000252).

Ames, Paul. "Belgium Links Arms Dealer, Al-Qaida." Associated Press report, 19 February 2002. <http://www.nitas.org>

Arostegui, Martin. "ETA Has Drugs-for-Weapons Deal with Mafia." United Press International report, 3 October 2002. <http://www.washtimes.com>

Babić, Jasna. "MORH Protects Arms Dealers Who Smuggle Weapons to ETA and IRA," *Nacional* [Zagreb], 24 July 2002 (FBIS Document EUP20010724000372).

"Bosnia Suspends Military Exports," Voice of America online report, 29 October 2002. <http://www.voanews.com>

Burgess, Mark. "Globalizing Terrorism: The FARC-IRA Connection." Center for Defense Information report, 5 June 2002. <http://www.cdi.org/terrorism/farc-ira-pr.cfm>

"Central and Eastern Europe Remains Important Source and Transit Route for Arms." <http://www.saferworld.uk>

Chiariello, Paolo, and Gian Antonio Orighi. "ETA and Camorra Crime Syndicate," *Panorama* [Milan], 3 October 2002 (FBIS Document EUP20020927000203).

Cowan, Rosie. "The 78 Criminal Gangs Waging War on Ulster," *The Guardian* [London], 23 March 2001.

Derix, Steven, and Jos Verlaan. "Investigative Services Want More Operational Powers at Schiphol," *NRC Handelsblad* [Rotterdam], 29 July 2002 (FBIS Document EUP20020730000226).

Evans, Richard. "Organised Crime and Terrorist Financing in Northern Ireland," *Jane's Intelligence Review*, 15 August 2002. <http://www.janes.com>

Federation of American Scientists, Intelligence Resource Program. "Basque Fatherland and Liberty, Euzkadi Ta Askatasuna (ETA)." <http://www.fas.org/irp/world/para/eta>

Federation of American Scientists, Intelligence Resource Program. "Irish Republican Army, Provisional Irish Republican Army (PIRA), the Provos, Direct Action Against Drugs (DAAD)." <http://www.fas.org/irp/world/para/ira>

Federation of American Scientists, Intelligence Resource Program. "Kurdistan Workers' Party (PKK)." <http://www.fas.org/irp/world/para/pkk>

Federation of American Scientists, Intelligence Resource Program. "New Irish Republican Army (NIRA), Real IRA, Óglaigh na hÉireann (Volunteers of Ireland)." <http://www.fas.org/irp/world/para/nira>

Germany. Generalbundesanwalt. "Indictment of Two Alleged Leading PKK Functionaries" (FBIS Document EUP20021029000049).

Graduate Institute of International Studies. *Small Arms Survey 2002*. Oxford and New York: Oxford University Press, 2002.

Harndon, Toby. "Adams Ally's Trade in Terror," *The Daily Telegraph* [London], 15 May 2002 (FBIS Document EUP20020515000149).

Harndon, Toby. "Farc Money Funded Arms Deals," *The Daily Telegraph* [London], 15 May 2002. <http://www.nitas.org>

"Israeli Arms Trafficker on Trial in Italy for Arms Sale to Liberia, Sierra Leone," Radio France Internationale [Paris] report based on story in *Corriere della Sera* [Milan], 19 June 2002 (FBIS Document AFP20020619000123).

Kahl, Murray, and Naji N. Najjar. "The Syrian Mafia Connection." <http://www/free-lebanon.com>

Kavain, Mario. "Did Colonel Zulu Arm IRA and ETA Terrorists from the Warehouse at Kaznjenička Battalion?" *Jutarnji List* [Zagreb], 18 August 2001 (FBIS Document EUP20010820000136).

Lallemand, Alaian. "Activities in Belgium," *Le Soir* [Brussels], 7 March 2002. <http://www.nisat.org>

Lallemand, Alaian. "A Belgian Angolagate?" *Le Soir* [Brussels], 16 June 2001. <http://www.nitas.org>

Lumpe, Lora, ed. *Running Guns: The Global Black Market in Small Arms*. New York: Zed Books, 2000.

McDermott, Jeremy, and Toby Harnden. "The IRA and the Colombian Connection." *The Daily Telegraph* [London], 15 August 2001. <http://www.nitas.org>

McMahon, Robert. "Afghanistan: UN Official Describes Effort to Track Al-Qaeda," Radio Free Europe/Radio Liberty online report, 28 January 2002. <http://www.rferl.org>

McMahon, Robert. "Yugoslavia: Arms Expert Traces Belgrade-to-Liberia Arms Trafficking," Radio Free Europe/Radio Liberty online report, 1 November 2002. <http://www.rferl.org>

Makarenko, Tamara. "Systematic Transnational Crime," *Jane's Intelligence Review*, 1 January 2002.

Metdepenningen, Marc. "Jacques Monsieur Hopes for Release," *Le Soir* [Brussels], 12 October 2002 (FBIS Document EUP20021013000011).

"Miraculous Weapon and Its Author," *Military Parade,* no. 3, 2002, 32.

Nikolakopoulos, V. "The Arms Trade in Greece," *To Vima tis Kiriakis* [Athens], 5 August 2001, cited by International Action Network on Small Arms. <http://www.iansa.org>

Observatoire Géopolitique des Drogues. *The World Geopolitics of Drugs 1998-1999": Annual Report*. Dordrecht: Kluwer, 2001.

Passas, Nikos. "Globalization and Transnational Crime: Effects of Criminogenic Asymmetries. Pages 22-56 in Phil Williams and Dimitri Vlassis, eds., *Combating Transnational Crime: Concepts, Activities and Responses*. London: Frank Cass, 2001.

Pasternak, Judy, and Stephen Braun. "Following the Trail of Arms to Al-Qaida," *Los Angeles Times*, 21 January 2002. <http://www.nisat.org>

Roule, T. "The Terrorist Financial Network of the PKK," *Jane's Terrorism and Security Monitor*, 17 June 2002.

Scepanovic, Ivo. "Arms Smuggling: Four Suspects Released," *The Irish News* [Belfast], 17 October 2002 (FBIS Document 20021017000122).

Simons, Marlise. "Balkan Gangs Stepping Up Violence, Dutch Say," *New York Times*, 30 November 2000. <http://www.nitas.org>

"Slovene Police Uncover Group of Arms, Drug Traffickers." Slovenian Press Agency report, 23 April 2001.

Sombolos, Yeoryios. “2.5 Billion Drachmas Annual Turnover from Arms Trafficking,” *Imerisia* [Athens], 22 December 2001. <http:www.nisat.org>

“Some 400,000 Illegal Weapons in Circulation in Greece,” *To Vima* [Athens], 19 April 2001 (FBIS Document GMP20010419000074).

“Tentacles into Greece,” *Ta Nea* [Athens], 20 July 2000. <http://www.nisat.org>

Traynor, Ian. “The International Dealers in Death,” *The Guardian* [London], 9 July 2001. <http://www.nisat.org>

Tremlett, Giles. “Karadzić Family ‘Arming Real IRA,’” *The Guardian* [Manchester], 5 April 2001. <http://www.nitas.org>

“Turkey Lifts Provincial Restrictions,” *Los Angeles Times*, 1 December 2002.

“UN Investigates Links of Belgian Diamond Dealers with Afghan Terrorism,” *Le Soir* [Brussels], 14 March 2002. <http://www.nitas.org>

U.S. Congress. House. Committee on International Relations. “Investigative Findings on the Activities of the Irish Republican Army (IRA) in Colombia,” 24 April 2002. <http://www.neoliberalismo.com/ira-farc>

U.S. Department of State. *Patterns of Global Terrorism 2001*. Washington, D.C.: 2001.

Verlaan, Jos. “Yugos Dominate Netherlands Arms Market,” *NRC Handelsblad* [Rotterdam], 5 July 2002 (FBIS Document EUP20020708000079).

Wilkinson, Isambard and Julius Strauss. “Karadzić Associates ‘Exporting Weapons,’” *The Daily Telegraph* [London], 19 April 2001.

Williams, Phil. “Drugs and Guns,” *Bulletin of the Atomic Scientists*, 55, no. 1 (January-February 1999). <http://www.bullatomsci.org>

Williams, Phil. “Organizing Transnational Crime: Networks, Markets and Hierarchies.” Pages 57-87 in Phil Williams and Dimitri Vlassis, eds. *Combating Transnational Crime: Concepts, Activities and Responses*. London: Frank Cass, 2001.

Wood, Brian, and Johan Peleman. *The Arms Fixers*. Report for Norwegian Initiative on Small Arms Transfers, 1999. <http://www.nisat.org>

“World’s Drug Traffickers Are Thriving on Globalization, Privatization,” Agence France Presse, 20 April 2000. <http://www.commondreams.org>

Wrase, Michael, and Waltraud Kaserer. "Belgrade Smuggled Weapons to Iraq," *Welt am Sonntag* [Hamburg], 27 October 2002 (FBIS Document EUP20021027000097).

Živak, V. "B-H Firms Sold Military Equipment to Burma, Libya," *Oslobođenje* [Sarajevo], 1 November 2002 (FBIS Document EUP20021101000224).

www.ingramcontent.com/pod-product-compliance
Lightning Source LLC
Chambersburg PA
CBHW080735290526
45790CB00008B/3201

* 9 7 8 1 4 8 1 9 2 1 2 8 2 *